W9-BGE-216

3 2224 00111 4923

Kids in the Kitchen™
The Library of Multicultural Cooking

Food and Recipes
of the Caribbean

by Theresa M. Beatty

The Rosen Publishing Group's
PowerKids Press™
New York

The recipes in this book are intended for a child to make together with an adult.
Many thanks to Ruth Rosen and her test kitchen.

Published in 1999 by The Rosen Publishing Group, Inc.
29 East 21st Street, New York, NY 10010

First Edition

Book Design: Resa Listort

Photo Credits and Photo Illustrations: p. 7 © Greg Johnston/International Stock; pp. 8, 14, 18 © John Novajosky; pp. 9, 19, 21 © Pablo Maldonado; pp. 10, 14 © 1995 PhotoDisc Inc.; p. 11 © Don Herbert/FPG International; p.13 © Ron Chapple/FPG International; p. 15 © J. P. Degas/Viesti Associates Inc.; p. 17 © Peter Gridley/FPG International; p. 20 © Michael Ventura/International Stock.

Beatty, Theresa M.
    Food and recipes of the Caribbean/by Theresa M. Beatty.
        p.   cm. — (Kids in the kitchen:multicultural cooking)
    Includes index.
    Summary: Describes some of the foods enjoyed in Jamaica, Cuba, and other islands in the Caribbean region and provides recipes for several popular Caribbean dishes.
    ISBN 0-8239-5221-5
    1. Cookery, Caribbean—Juvenile literature. 2. Food habits—Caribbean Area—Juvenile literature. [1. Food Habits—Caribbean Area. 2. Cookery, Caribbean.] I. Title. II. Series: Beatty, Theresa M. Kids in the kitchen.
    TX716.A1B43   1998
    641.59729—dc21   97-11212
                                                                                                            CIP
                                                                                                            AC

Manufactured in the United States of America

CONTENTS

Abbreviations

cup = c. Farenheit = F. tablespoon = tbsp. teaspoon = tsp.

Celsius = C. kilogram = kilo liter = l milliliter = ml

The Caribbean

The clear, blue waters of the Caribbean Sea run along the northern coast of South America and the eastern coast of Central America. Cuba, Jamaica, Puerto Rico, and Hispaniola are the largest of about 30 islands in the Caribbean. Hispaniola is the island that has Haiti and the Dominican Republic on it. The areas of Mexico, South America, and Central America that are close to the Caribbean Sea are also part of the Caribbean.

Because the Caribbean is made up of many countries with different **cultures** (KUL-cherz), there are a great number of cooking styles.

The islands of the Caribbean were first called the West Indies because they were originally thought to be part of India.

5

Caribbean Cuisine

Over time, other cultures have helped shape Caribbean **cuisine** (kwih-ZEEN). After Christopher Columbus visited the Caribbean in 1493, people from Spain, France, Holland, Denmark, and Britain **settled** (SEH-tuld) on many of the islands. The cooking styles of the European settlers were mixed with those of the islands' natives, such as the Arawaks and the Caribs. The fruits and vegetables of the area gave the cuisine of the Caribbean its unique flavor.

Caribbean cooks season a lot of their food before cooking it. The Caribbean **climate** (KLY-mit) is hot. Long ago, people didn't have refrigerators to keep foods cold and fresh. Caribbean cooks used spices to help food stay fresh and to cover up bad flavors.

Like the cuisine, the homes in the Caribbean are very colorful.

African Influence

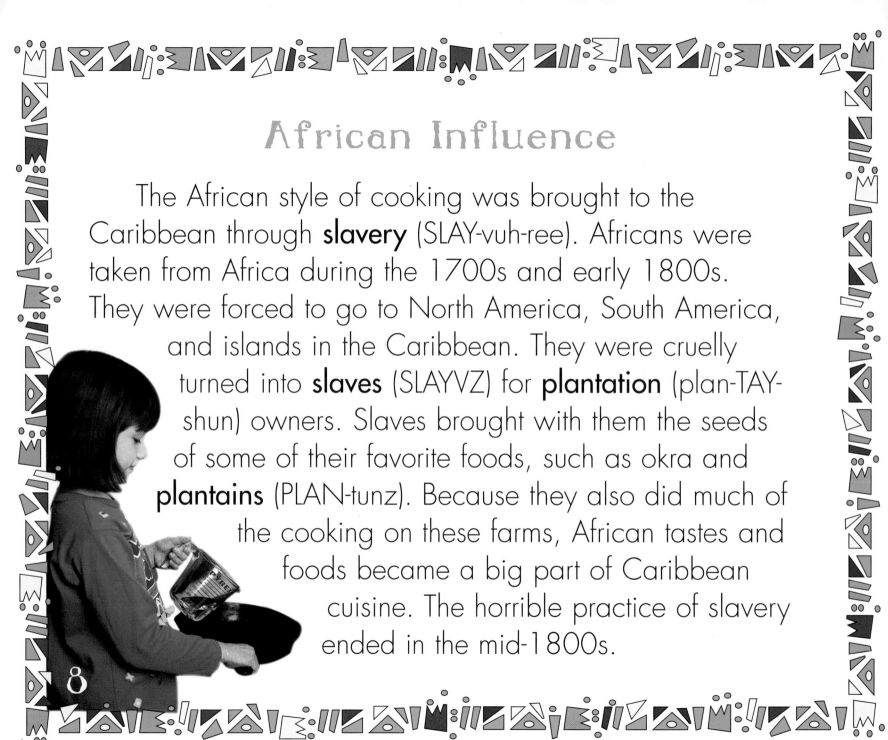

The African style of cooking was brought to the Caribbean through **slavery** (SLAY-vuh-ree). Africans were taken from Africa during the 1700s and early 1800s. They were forced to go to North America, South America, and islands in the Caribbean. They were cruelly turned into **slaves** (SLAYVZ) for **plantation** (plan-TAY-shun) owners. Slaves brought with them the seeds of some of their favorite foods, such as okra and **plantains** (PLAN-tunz). Because they also did much of the cooking on these farms, African tastes and foods became a big part of Caribbean cuisine. The horrible practice of slavery ended in the mid-1800s.

Fried Plantains

2 unripe (green)
    plantains or green
    bananas
olive oil or vegetable
    oil

HOW TO DO IT:

- Peel and slice plantains into thin slices and place in a bowl.
- Cover a plate with a few paper towels and set aside.
- Pour just enough olive oil in a frying pan to cover bottom.
- Heat oil over medium-high heat.
- Place several plantain slices in pan.
- Fry until slices begin to turn golden on each side, about 3 minutes, turning as needed.
- Remove from pan and place on plate with paper towels to absorb extra oil.

Serves 4

Always ask a grown-up to help you when using knives!
Always ask a grown-up to help you when using the stove or oven!

Caribbean Food

Plantains are found all over the Caribbean. This fruit looks a lot like the banana, but it is usually cooked before it is eaten. The British brought the popular breadfruit from Tahiti to the Caribbean. It is kind of like a potato, but it's a bit sweeter.

Have you ever tried a guava fruit? What about genips or mangoes? **Tropical** (TRAH-pih-kul) fruits like these, along with bananas, coconuts, and pineapples, grow all over the Caribbean.

Because Caribbean countries are surrounded by water, seafood is a part of most meals. Crab, grouper, and red snapper are all popular.

Fishermen and fisherwomen on the island of St. Vincent use nets to catch fish that they eat or sell. ▶

Jamaica

The beautiful island of Jamaica has green mountains and sunny white-sand beaches. It is the third largest Caribbean island and a popular place for people to visit. The food and **customs** (KUS-tumz) of Jamaica lend a lot to Caribbean culture.

Jamaica's national dish is saltfish and **ackee** (AH-kee). Saltfish is cod that is specially prepared with salt. Ackee is a West African fruit that was brought to Jamaica in the 1700s. Ackee looks and tastes like scrambled eggs. Jamaicans are careful with this fruit and you should be too. Ackees are ripe only when the fruit turns red and splits open. If you eat an ackee that is not ripe, you could get sick.

People visit Jamaica to enjoy the beaches, such as this one at Dunn's River Falls, and taste original Jamaican cuisine.

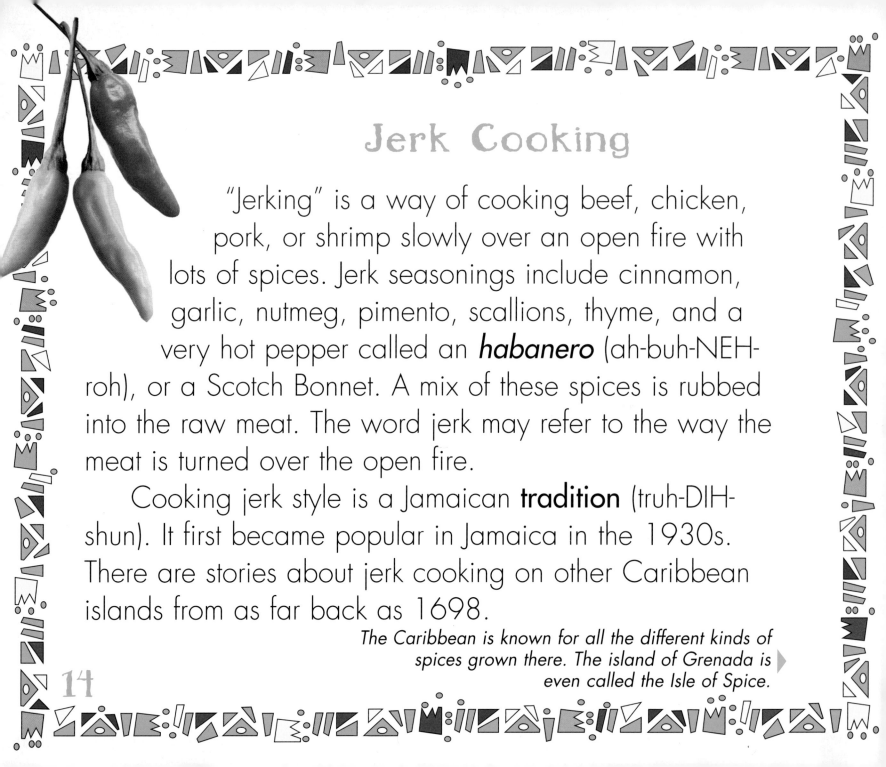

Jerk Cooking

"Jerking" is a way of cooking beef, chicken, pork, or shrimp slowly over an open fire with lots of spices. Jerk seasonings include cinnamon, garlic, nutmeg, pimento, scallions, thyme, and a very hot pepper called an **habanero** (ah-buh-NEH-roh), or a Scotch Bonnet. A mix of these spices is rubbed into the raw meat. The word jerk may refer to the way the meat is turned over the open fire.

Cooking jerk style is a Jamaican **tradition** (truh-DIH-shun). It first became popular in Jamaica in the 1930s. There are stories about jerk cooking on other Caribbean islands from as far back as 1698.

The Caribbean is known for all the different kinds of spices grown there. The island of Grenada is even called the Isle of Spice.

The Cayman Islands

The three Cayman Islands are northwest of Jamaica. The Cayman Islands are known for great scuba diving, colorful fish, and big turtles.

A popular food in the Cayman Islands is the **conch** (KONK). This large, pink sea snail lives in a spiral shell. Once the meat is removed from the shell, people often use the shell as a kind of horn. A conch shell can make loud, musical sounds when someone blows through it.

The people of the Cayman Islands cook conch many different ways. Conch stew is made with onions, coconut milk, and, of course, spices. Conch fritters are bits of conch meat dipped in batter and then fried. Conch is also prepared jerk style.

Some people like to eat raw conch. ▶

Cuban Cooking

The island of Cuba is only 90 miles from Key West, Florida, in the United States. Because of this, many Cubans have moved to the United States, bringing with them their special cuisine. In fact, Miami, Florida, is known for its great Cuban restaurants.

Much of the Cuban style of cooking comes from Spain. In 1511 Spanish settlers drove the native Arawak people from their island. The Spanish settled there, bringing their ways of cooking with them.

Cubans use an adobo **marinade** (MA-rih-nayd) of chili peppers, paprika, and vinegar that is like what is used in Spain today.

18

Caribbean Rice

You will need:

2 tbsp. *(30 ml)* vegetable or olive oil

1 c. *(250 ml)* uncooked rice

½ clove garlic, crushed

1 tsp. *(5 ml)* turmeric

1 tsp. *(5 ml)* dried thyme

1 tsp. *(5 ml)* salt

⅛ tsp. *(½ ml)* allspice

½ tsp. *(2 ml)* black pepper

1 green pepper, chopped

1 medium onion, chopped

2 c. *(500 ml)* hot chicken broth

¼ c. *(50 ml)* fresh cilantro, chopped or 1 tsp. *(5 ml)* dried cilantro

½ c. *(125 ml)* scallions, chopped

2 tbsp. *(30 ml)* lime juice

HOW TO DO IT:

- Heat oil in a medium-sized saucepan over medium-high heat.
- When oil is hot, add rice, garlic, turmeric, thyme, salt, allspice, black pepper, green pepper, and onion.
- Cook for 3–4 minutes, stirring often.
- Add chicken broth and continue to stir.
- Bring to a boil.
- Lower heat and cover. Let simmer for about 15 minutes, or until the rice is soft.
- Remove from heat and let covered pot stand for about 8 minutes.
- Add scallions, lime juice, and cilantro. Stir well.

Serves 4

Always ask a grown-up to help you when using knives!
Always ask a grown-up to help you when using the stove or oven!

Carnival

Carnival is a time of great fun in the Caribbean. It takes place during the six weeks before Lent. Lent is a special time for Christian people in which they prepare for Easter. During carnival, parades of masked people dance through the streets in shiny costumes made of feathers and brightly colored cloth. This **festival** (FES-tih-vul) usually takes place in February or March.

Trinidad has one of the largest **celebrations** (SEL-uh-BRAY-shunz) of all the Caribbean islands. Food is cooked and served everywhere at carnival. *Pastelitos* (pah-stel-EE-tohs), made of flavored meat or cheese wrapped in plantain dough, can be bought at stands in the street.

20

Island Sugar Cakes

You will need:

3½ c. (875 ml) grated coconut or packaged coconut flakes

¾ c. (175 ml) water

¾ c. (175 ml) sugar

½ tsp. (2 ml) cream of tartar

1 tsp. (5 ml) almond extract

3–4 drops red or green food coloring

HOW TO DO IT:

- In a medium saucepan, bring sugar and water to a boil over medium-high heat.
- Add coconut and cream of tartar and stir.
- Continue to heat, watching mixture closely.
- Remove from heat when mixture no longer sticks to sides of pan.
- Beat for 3 to 5 minutes with a spoon.
- Add food coloring and almond extract. Mix well.
- Drop by spoonfuls onto a greased cookie sheet.
- Repeat until all of mixture is used.
- Allow balls to harden.
- Store in an airtight container.

Makes 28 cakes

Always ask a grown-up to help you when using knives!
Always ask a grown-up to help you when using the stove or oven!

Caribbean Food Outside the Caribbean

The flavors of Caribbean cooking have become popular in many places throughout the world. The state of Louisiana in the United States is famous for its Cajun and Creole cooking. Creole cuisine has been influenced by French and Spanish cooking styles. But ingredients from the Caribbean are found in Creole recipes also.

The one-pot stews that are so popular in Africa and the Caribbean are popular throughout the world. Gumbo, a one-pot stew that gets its name from an African word for okra, is a dish found in African American and Cajun cooking.

Using the recipes in this book, you can bring the tastes of the Caribbean to the people you know.

Glossary

ackee (AH-kee) A popular fruit brought to Jamaica from West Africa.

celebration (SEL-uh-BRAY-shun) A special time honoring something that is enjoyed with a gathering.

climate (KLY-mit) The weather conditions of a certain place.

conch (KONK) A snail-like fish that lives in a large shell.

cuisine (kwih-ZEEN) A style of cooking.

culture (KUL-cher) The beliefs, customs, art, and religion of a group of people.

custom (KUS-tum) The accepted, respected way of doing something that is passed down from parent to child.

festival (FES-tih-vul) A day or special time of recognizing someone or something important.

habanero (ah-buh-NEH-roh) A hot pepper used in jerk seasoning.

marinade (MA-rih-nayd) A way of flavoring food, usually meat, with spices or sauces before cooking.

pastelito (pah-stel-EE-toh) Meat or cheese wrapped in plantain dough.

plantain (PLAN-tun) A banana-like fruit.

plantation (plan-TAY-shun) A large farm on which crops, such as cotton, tobacco, sugarcane, and rubber trees, are grown.

settle (SEH-tul) To move from another country to a new land to live.

slave (SLAYV) A person who is "owned" by another person and is forced to work for them.

slavery (SLAY-vuh-ree) The system of one person "owning" another.

tradition (truh-DIH-shun) A way of doing something that is passed down through a family.

tropical (TRAH-pih-kul) Very hot and humid.

Index